GW01057457

What is Faith?

Faith for Healing   **Faith for Victory**

Faith to Receive God's Promises

Faith for the Baptism   **Faith to Overcome**

in the Holy Spirit   **Satan**

Faith to Overcome Doubt

Table of Contents

INTRODUCTION

This book is a humble attempt to bring forth a comprehensive look at the topic of faith in a short easy to read format.

A large portion of this book is not original material written by myself. It was written by Dr. Horbart Freeman during his early years of pastoring Faith Assembly Church in Warsaw, IN. However, I have added, deleted and changed some of the contents as I deemed appropriate based upon my study of the Scriptures and 25 years of ministry experience.

Since Dr. Freeman's book was not under copyright, and because an understanding of faith is significant to both new believers as well as the more mature Christian who may need a reminder of the foundational principles of faith, I decided to re-write his book.

I have also prepared this small book to encourage the Body of Christ to return to a greater walk of faith (trust in God) with less reliance on the world.

I sincerely hope you find it informative and helpful.

Sincerely,

Jim Fent

The only cost for this book is what is required by the company who prints and distributes it. Any small amount I may receive will go to supplying books to those who cannot afford to purchase one.

CHAPTER ONE

What Is Faith?

The scriptural definition of faith is stated in Hebrews 11:1. "Now faith is the substance of things hoped for, the evidence of things not seen." Biblical faith contains two elements; *substance* and *evidence.*

The word *"substance"* is an excellent translation of the Greek word *"hupostasis"* used in Hebrews 11:1 because it literally means *that which has real existence, the actual reality, and the substance of something.* Therefore, your faith is something real. It is the "substance" of that which you hope for.

So what does this mean? It means that if you, by faith, appropriate (ask for) a promise which God declares in His Word, and if you believe that you receive it when you prayed (Mk. 11:24), then your faith stands in the place of what you asked for until it manifests visibly.

Your faith takes the place of what you asked for as an invisible, but nevertheless real, substance until the thing you requested is made visible in your sight; then, faith is no longer needed.

So faith is the substance (the reality) of things hoped for. It is as real in the sight of God as the thing you asked for will be to you when you see it manifested.

Faith is also *"evidence."* Faith is the evidence of things not seen. Evidence of anything is ABSOLUTE PROOF of its reality and existence. This means that the very fact that you have faith that God has heard and granted your request is evidence that you have received what you do not yet see. You have received it by faith.

When you know in your heart that your request has been answered before you see it, your faith is the evidence that you have it. On the other hand, if you merely have hope then there is no evidence, because hope is mingled with doubt, fear and anxiety to whether or not you will receive what you ask for.

When genuine faith is in your heart you know that God has granted your petition when you ask, and this faith (heart knowledge) is your evidence that you have what you do not **yet** see. Jesus said, "...whatever things you ask when you pray, believe that you have received them". (Mark 11:24).

- In the Greek it actually says, "Believe that you have (already) received them".

Faith is all that you need to appropriate all of God's promises and make them a reality in your life. Everything God has declared in Scripture has already been accomplished because Jesus did it on the cross. Therefore, we do not have to ask God to do something He has already done, we just need to appropriate (ask for) it for ourselves and others. In other words, we are not to pray the problem but rather we are to pray the promise (His Word). Faith simply says to speak it and believe it.

Whatever we speak is critical to our wellbeing. Speak something negative or contrary to God's Word and Satan will take your words and accuse you before God (Rev.

12:10-11). But if you declare God's Word, His promises, then Satan has nothing by which to accuse you.

What faith is not, is hope. Faith is the means by which we receive those things hoped for. Neither is faith sight. Faith is the evidence of things not seen. Faith can only operate in the realm of the invisible.

CHAPTER TWO

Scriptural Evidence of Faith for Healing

The principles of faith presented in this book apply to any promise God has made to the believer in His Word (The Bible). However, the two greatest needs in the Body of Christ today are for bodily healing and deliverance from demonic influences and infestations. The latter is explained in detail in the book entitled "Breaking Chains of Darkness" (www.lulu.com/spotlight/jfent). Therefore, because the need for bodily healing from disease and affliction is so great the topic of healing will be given special attention.

This short chapter is specifically designed for those who are not well grounded in the teachings of scripture concerning the promises of God for the healing of our diseases and illnesses in Christ's Atonement.

However, prior to looking at scriptural passages that express this truth it is imperative that we first correct any unscriptural notion held by many that God is the Author of sickness, which He sends to us as a "blessing in disguise," to patiently endure for His glory. This cannot be supported by scripture and is in direct conflict with God's Word concerning faith. As long as this idea prevails in one's mind, they are unable to exercise their faith for healing.

If God had actually sent you a disease or illness as a "blessing" or a "correction" then it would be a sin to seek its removal by medicines or treatment by doctors. Yet all who are sick and believe it is from God still seek to be healed either by prayer or medical treatment.

The key here is to understand that for you to receive faith for healing you must first understand that *the Scriptures teach that all pain, sickness and disease are from Satan* (see Job 2:6-7; Luke 13:10-16; I Corinthians 5:5; Acts 10:38).

Also compare the many instances in the Gospels in which Jesus healed the diseased and afflicted by casting out demons, thereby, overcoming the work of Satan. Jesus healed all the sick who came in faith unto Him (Matt. 8:16).

Look at the Scriptures

It is strongly suggested that you do a sincere study of the passages of scripture where this truth of healing is taught in order to strengthen your faith and remove any doubts you may have.

If God has actually provided for, and promised us, healing for the body in the atonement of Christ, then we should be able to find this truth in His Word (The Bible). If we can find it, then we have assurance that it is God's will to heal all who will exercise faith, because faith comes by hearing and believing God's Word.

If sincere consideration of the following passages does not lead to a belief that God has promised you healing for your sicknesses as well as your sins, then it would be futile to attempt to support this truth by argument. Therefore, the passages are presented here with minimal or no comment because anyone who humbly seeks the truth of the validity of this doctrine will see it clearly; those who have prejudged the question in the negative on the basis of theological background, prejudice, or rationale argument, will most likely not be able to receive it.

Please read the following passages:

Isaiah 53:4: "Surely He has borne our grief's and carried our sorrows." Literally in the Hebrew it says, "Surely He has carried away our diseases, and borne our pains."

Matt. 8:16-17: "When evening had come, they brought to Him many who were sick and demon-possessed. And He cast out the spirits with a word and healed all who were sick, that it might be fulfilled which was spoken by Isaiah the prophet, saying: He Himself took our infirmities and bore our sicknesses."

Isaiah 53:5: "…He was wounded for our transgressions, He was bruised for our iniquities; the chastisement of our peace was upon Him. And by His stripes we are healed."

Exodus 15:26: "If you diligently heed the voice of the Lord your God and do what is right in His sight, give ear to His commandments and keep all His statutes (laws), I will put none of the diseases on you which I have brought on the Egyptians. For I am the Lord who heals you.

Exodus 23:25: "So you shall serve the Lord your God, and He will bless your bread and your water. And I will take sickness away from the midst of you."

Psalm 103:3: "Who forgives all your iniquities and heals all your diseases."

Deuteronomy 7:15: "And the Lord will take away from you all sickness…."

Mark 16:17-18: "And these signs will follow those who believe: In My name they will cast out demons, they will speak with new tongues; they will take up serpents (reference to Acts 28:3-5); and if they drink anything deadly, it will by no means hurt them; they will lay hands on the sick, and they will recover."

James 5:14-16: "And the prayer of faith will save the sick, and the Lord will raise him up. And if he has committed sins, he will be forgiven. Confess your trespasses to one another, and pray for one another, that you may be healed. The effective, fervent prayer of a righteous man avails much."

I Peter 2:24: "Who Himself (Jesus) bore our sins in His own body on the tree, that we, having died to sin, might live for righteousness----by whose stripes *you were* healed."

III John 2: "Beloved I pray that you prosper (in the truth of God) in all things and be in health, just as your soul prospers."

Mark 11:22-24: "...have faith (trust) in God. For assuredly, I say to you, whoever says to this mountain, 'Be removed and be cast into the sea; and does not doubt in his heart, but believes that those things he says will come to pass, he will have whatever he says.' Therefore, I say to you, *whatever things you ask when you pray, believe that you receive them, and you will have them.*"

Matthew 21:22: "...whatever you ask in prayer, *believing,* you will receive."

Acts 9:34: "And Peter said to him, 'Aeneas, Jesus the Christ heals you. Arise and make you bed.' Then he rose immediately."

Matthew 8:10: "Then His fame went out throughout all Syria; and they brought to Him all who were afflicted with various diseases and torments, and those who were demon possessed, epileptics, and paralytics; and He healed them."

CHAPTER THREE

How to Receive God's Promises By Faith

Everything that God promises in His Word (Bible) can be received by an act of faith. This is true concerning salvation *(Jn. 3:16; Rom. 10:9-10)*; physical healing *(Mt. 9:22; Jam. 5:15)*; the baptism in the Holy Spirit (Lk 11:13; Acts 2:38-39; Gal. 3:2, 14); the provision of our material needs (Mt. 624-30, note vs 30); or whatever particular need and/or problem we may have.

By faith we are justified (Rom. 3:28); sanctified (Acts 26:18); and preserved (I Peter 1:5). By faith we overcome Satan (Eph. 6:16) and the world (I Jn. 5:4). By faith we have access to God (Rom. 5:2); inherit the promises of God (Heb. 6:12); stand (II Cor. 1:24); walk (II Cor. 5:7); live (Gal. 2:20); and die (Heb. 11:13). The central importance of faith in the life of the believer is clearly set forth in God's Word, because we are told that *"without faith it is impossible to please Him* (Heb. 11:6); and *"whatever is not from faith is sin"* (Rom. 14:23). Nothing a Christian has, is, hopes to accomplish, obtain, or become, is possible apart from an active faith.

In reality Christians are rich spiritually, materially, and physically, but very few are aware of this fact, believing instead that we don't receive our inheritance in the present life but only in the life to come. The Scriptures, on the contrary, declare that our inheritance belongs to us NOW, because God promises that "all things are yours...whether the world, or life or death, or things present, or things to come; all are yours" (I Coe. 3:21-22). <u>God has given us all things</u> in Christ Jesus now as joint-heirs with Him (Rom. 8:16-17; Gal. 4:5-7). He is saying that all things are yours now—<u>in the world, in life, in your present, as well as in death and the life to come.</u>

If all things are yours in the present as well as in the future, then this means that you can enter into your inheritance right now IF you will exercise your faith to appropriate them. They are not automatic: you must receive them by faith (ask and believe).

Jesus purchased all rights, privileges, wealth, dominion, power and authority in the universe by His redemption at Calvary. They belong to Him now. You are a joint-heir with Him and seated with Him in the heavens (Eph. 2:5-6) and are authorized to claim all these things by faith; now as well as in the world to come. It is your inheritance and it does not have to begged or pleaded for, God does not have to be persuaded, "for all the promises of God in Him (Christ) are yes and amen" (II Cor. 1:20). God not only promises that all things are yours now, but in this verse He assures you that *He has already said "yes" to all that He promises to you even before you ask.* The answer is always yes to any promise God makes to you if you meet the condition of faith. This means then, that you have not because you ask not (Jam. 2:4). You do not ask because you either lack the faith to take God at His Word, or you do not know how to ask.

14

FIVE CONDITIONS OF FAITH

Ground Your Faith in the Word of God

The Apostle Paul declares that "faith comes by hearing and hearing by the Word of God" (Rom. 10:17). Hearing, knowing and more specifically BELIEVING the Word of God is the secret to faith. This is how we gain the faith needed to appropriate what God has promised to us and to do through us. Our faith cannot rise above what God has promised in His Word, either specifically or in principle. For example, *specific* promises are made to us in such passages as Matthew 6:33, James 5:15, Psalm 91, and Mark 16:17-20. The *principle* of faith embracing any problem, requirement or need is set forth in Mark 11:22-24 and Matthew 17:20. (A review of these verses will assist in building your faith).

Faith is believing that God will do for, in and through you what He promises in His Word. *Faith is believing God!* God and His Word are in one accord. Believing His Word is believing God. God will not fail to fulfill every promise which He makes to us for *"God is not a man, that He should lie; nor a son of man, that He should repent. He has said, and will He not do it? He has spoken, and will He not make it good?"* (Numbers 23:19).

The general lack of faith among Christians today is, I believe, primarily due to the fact that *they do not know* what God's Word promises them. The saints of the Old and New Testaments, including the prophets and apostles, were not supernaturally endowed with special faith more than any other believer (Jam. 5:15-18). They received their answers to prayer, and the empowering to work miracles and perform mighty acts for God, by fulfilling the condition necessary to acquire strong faith---*hearing and believing God's Word.*

Ask in Faith What Your Faith Can Believe in God's Word

The second condition is simply to ASK! *"Ask and it shall be given to you....For EVERYONE who asks receives."* Read Matthew 7:7-11

The promises of God are not automatic just because we believe them---we only receive what we specifically ask for in faith. We do not have to persuade God, He is ready and willing to accommodate our requests but we do have to ask. As stated in James 4:2, "You do not have because you do not ask."

God has already said "yes" to everything He promised even before you ask, therefore, the answer you seek can never be "no" when you ask in faith (believing). "And ALL things, whatever you ask in prayer, believing, you WILL receive" (Matt. 21:22).

Confess What You Believe and Have Requested By Faith

Verbal confession is your faith speaking. Confession is faith's way of expressing itself. *"For with the heart one believes...and with the mouth confession is made..."* (Rom. 10:10). If we truly believe that God will keep His promises to us, it will be expressed by what we say (confess).

Jesus in Mark 11:2 also emphasizes the significance between what we say and receiving what we ask for:

> "For assuredly, I say to you, whoever says to this Mountain, 'Be removed and be cast into the sea,' and does not doubt in his heart, but believes that those things he says will come to pass, he will receive whatever he says."

We receive what we speak and confess. This is why scripture places a strong emphasis on a positive confession (Matt. 10:32-33; I Tim. 6:12-13; Jam. 1:6-7; Mark 11:22-24). Scripture also says that if we speak negatively we will receive nothing (Jam. 1:6-7).

Let me share an example: Last night during a "revival" meeting the disease of diabetes was called out and a gentlemen responded to that call. He received prayer for healing of that disease. After the meeting he decided to stay for refreshments and was heard saying, "I am going to have a brownie because I was just healed of diabetes." That is a confession of faith.

So often we hear brothers and sisters in Christ preface things with a statement like "I just can't believe…whatever." That is not a good way to build your faith. Instead start making positive confessions and speak blessings rather than curses, because negative confession is doubt and doubt imprisons your faith and makes it impossible to release, because *"You are snared by the words of your mouth"*(Prov. 6:2).

Faith always speaks in agreement with God's Word. Why? Because this is the literal meaning of the verb "to confess" in the New Testament Greek: *homologeo"* means "to agree with," "to speak the same language," "to confess."

The Word of God declares that, "By His stripes you *were* healed" (Isa. 53:5). Believe it, confess it and continue in faith until you see it (until it manifests) and He promises His answer will be yes.

Act on Your Faith

There is a difference between heart faith and mere intellectual belief. Often people think they have genuine faith but fail to act on their faith. The scriptures show that when true faith is present it will produce works of faith, that is, corresponding actions. When Jesus anointed the blind man's eyes with clay and commanded him to wash in the pool of Siloam, this gave the man an opportunity to put his faith in action. James declares, "…that faith by itself, if it does not have works, is dead" (Jam. 2:17). In Mark 2:1-5 we read that Jesus "saw" the faith of the men who lowered the sick man with palsy down through the roof. Obviously, you cannot *see* faith---but you can see *faith at work!* It is to their faith in action that Jesus refers.

Genuine faith will always produce a corresponding action. All of the heroes in Hebrews chapter 11 are said to have done something which gave evidence of their faith. "By faith Able offered a more excellent sacrifice than Cain…by faith Noah prepared an Ark…by faith Abraham offered up Isaac…by faith Moses forsook Egypt, etc." When true faith is present we will always act on it.

Hold Fast until Your Request Has Manifested

Sometimes we do everything correctly, but when our request doesn't manifest quickly we began to waver and change our confession from speaking God's promise to speaking doubt. Scripture calls this being double-minded and a double-minded person receives nothing from the Lord (see James 1:6-8).

Surround yourself with others who can stand in faith with you and keep you in prayer. Their faith will help you maintain your faith between the time of request and the moment your request manifests.

CHAPTER FOUR

How To Receive The Baptism In The Holy Spirit By Faith

The Spirit received at conversion is like a cup filled to the top. Add the Baptism in the Holy Spirit and the cup over flows.

As previously mentioned, all of God's promises are appropriated by faith. Our faith cannot embrace anything which God does not promise in His Word. Therefore, we must always ground our faith in His Word.

The Baptism in the Holy Spirit is clearly promised to every believer in God's Word, but one cannot receive this empowering and blessing until he has gotten over any doubts or doctrinal questions about the possibility of being filled. To remove any doubts it is recommended that you study the passages related to the Baptism in the Holy Spirit and spend time discussing it with someone with a history of using this gift from God. If a humble sincere study and discussion of the scriptures does not quicken your faith for this experience, then all other arguments and examples would be superfluous.

This chapter is for (1) Those who have already gotten beyond the question of the validity of the Baptism, and desire it, but for various reasons have not yet received this experience with the accompanying sign of speaking in other tongues as the evidence; and (2) for those who question the scriptural evidence for speaking in other tongues: Those who may not be thoroughly grounded in the Scriptures with regard to this question, or who have erroneously taught to equate receiving the Holy Spirit in regeneration with the "baptism" in the Holy Spirit. Therefore, we will discuss the basic passage where the truth of the baptism is taught so you may study it in order to remove any doubts and create the faith needed to receive this blessing.

Study of the relevant passages will also indicate that certain terms and phrases are used synonymously with reference to the baptism in the Holy Spirit. The New Testament equates the following to each other: "The baptism in the Holy Spirit," "the gift of the Holy Spirit," "pouring out of the Spirit," "filled with the Spirit," "receiving the Spirit," etc. Compare for example, Acts 1:4-5 with 2:4; 10:45; 11:15-17, where the term "baptized," "filled," and "gift" are used synonymously.

The Promise

Old Testament Prophecy: Joel predicted that in the latter days (church age) God would pour out His Spirit upon all flesh: "And it shall come to pass afterward that I will pour out My Spirit on all flesh; Your sons and daughters will prophecy…"(Joel 2:28). This was first experienced on the Day of Pentecost, when 120 disciples were all filled with the Holy Spirit and spoke with new languages or tongues. But this evidence was not limited to this group of 120 as we see from Peter's words of explanation of their experience in Acts 2:38-39 where the same gift of the Holy Spirit is promised to all those who receive Christ *"for the promise is to you and your children, and to all who afar off, as many as the Lord will call."* The Promise of the baptism in the Holy Spirit is without question for *all believers* who will exercise the faith to appropriate (request) it.

New Testament Promise: The classic passage where Jesus offers us the gift of the Holy Spirit is Luke 11:9-13. Verse 13 reads: *If you then being evil, know how to give good gifts to your children, how much more will your heavenly Father give the Holy Spirit to those who ask Him!"* The willingness of our heavenly Father to give us the baptism in the Holy Spirit is clearly indicated here, since as a child of God, we already have the Spirit of regeneration (Rom. 8:9, 15-16).

The Evidence

Often I have heard questions like: "How do I know if I have received the Holy Spirit?" "Is there a scriptural sign that one has been filled with the Spirit?" I believe there is. However, some, for various reasons, have not wanted to speak in tongues, but say they believe the baptism in the Holy Spirit is a valid experience for today, claim they have received the baptism without speaking in tongues. They speak of an "inward experience," "of an anointing," "of being beside oneself with joy," "of feeling great strength of love" and so forth. But all of these so called evidences are based upon "feeling" or "emotion" of which the bible says nothing in regard to the baptism in the Holy Spirit. Yes, we are all human and have God given emotions that we definitely experience when we are in God's presence. However, we must evaluate these experiences in light of scripture; when we do this, we find that speaking in a new language or tongue supernaturally is the Scriptural sign or evidence of our receiving the baptism in the Holy Spirit.

Speaking in Tongues Was Predicted in the Old Testament

Joel 2:28-29: Peter quotes this to authenticate the divine source of their ability to speak the new languages at Pentecost. Joel had predicted the outpouring or baptism: Peter said the new tongues were the evidence or sign. Note carefully that it was the phenomenon of speaking in tongues that excited the Jews causing them to inquire: "What could this mean?"(Acts 2:12).

Isaiah 28:11-12. Paul cites this prophecy to indicate that speaking in tongues in the church had been predicted by Isaiah (see I Corinthians 14:21-22).

This Sign Was Incontestable Proof to the Jewish Church that the Holy Spirit Had Been Given to the Gentiles

Acts 10:44-45. It was when they heard them speak with tongues that Peter declares that they "have received the Holy Ghost as well as we." In Acts 11:16 he calls it the *"baptism in the Holy Ghost (Spirit)."*

This Sign Was Doubtless Missing from the Samaritans Experience. Thus it was Evident They Had Not Received the Baptism in the Holy Spirit

Acts 8:4-8, 12-19. Moreover, verse 18 says that Simon "saw" something which caused him to offer money for the power to give the Holy Spirit to others. Neither Phillip's healings, deliverance (exorcism), nor miracles caused him to offer money for these. Evidently he had heard them speaking in tongues when they received the baptism in the Holy Spirit.

The 120 Disciples "All" Spoke With New Tongues and They Accepted This Alone as Evidence That Christ Had Fulfilled His Promise to Baptize Them in the Holy Spirit.

Compare Acts 1:4-5, 8 with Acts 2:4, 2:33. This is their own interpretation of their experience; namely, that the baptism in the Holy Spirit results in speaking in tongues.

Twenty Years After Pentecost Speaking in Tongues Was Still the Sign and Evidence of Receiving the Holy Spirit.

Acts 19:1-6

Speaking in Tongues Was a Commonly Accepted Phenomenon in the Churches and Considered a Manifestation of the Holy Spirit

I Corinthians 12:14; Romans 8:26-27; Ephesians 6:18; Jude 20.

We can conclude, therefore, that speaking in tongues and this alone can be the Scriptural evidence confirming the baptism in the Holy Spirit.

God would not base the assurance of having given us the Holy Spirit on mere feelings or an emotional experience no matter how precious or sacred these may be to us individually. He chose to use speaking in other tongues supernaturally as the evidence of the baptism because it is (1) outward evidence; (2) uniform evidence; (3) universal evidence; and (4) supernatural evidence. Emotional, physical, or spiritual manifestations may also occur, and sometimes do accompany the sign of tongues, but the bible does not tell us to look for them because they are unreliable and variable. We are to look for the sign God has given:

"These signs will follow them that believe.........
They shall speak in new tongues." (Acts 16:17).

How to Receive the Baptism in the Holy Spirit

The conditions for receiving the baptism in the Holy Spirit by faith are essentially the same as receiving anything God has promised to the believer in His Word. These are the five conditions previous outlined in Chapter Three: They are: (1) Base your faith on the Word, (2) Ask; (3) Confess or speak it; (4) Act on your faith; and (5) Standing without doubting.

You may receive the baptism either by the laying on of hands or through your own personal prayer of faith. In either event the conditions are the same.

Too often believer's receive the baptism in the Holy Spirit with the evidence of speaking in tongues but fail to continue using this most powerful gift. For those who do not have a solid biblical understanding of the purposes and benefits of speaking in other tongues you are encouraged to read the author's booklet entitled "Tongues of Fire." (see www.lulu.com/spotlight/jfent)

CHAPTER FIVE

How To Overcome Doubt By Faith

Have you ever wondered why it is that your prayers are seldom answered? Or why you were not healed although you thought you prayed in faith? Or why there is so much defeat and worry in your life instead of joy, peace and victory which Christians are supposed to have? Have you ever wondered why your faith is so weak and inadequate? Do trials cause your faith to languish and grow faint rather than strong and mature?

The Word of God gives you the reason. It is **doubt**! The temptation to doubt what God has promised in His Word is one of Satan's most effect weapons to rob Christians of peace of mind, healing, joy, material provision of his needs, spiritual power, strong faith, blessings and victory. The spiritual principle set forth in James 1:5-7 is applicable to any situation or promise God has made us in His Word which is appropriated by faith.

> If any one of you lacks wisdom, let him ask God
> who gives to all liberally and without reproach,
> and it will be given to him. But let him ask in faith,
> with no doubting, for he who doubts is like a wave
> of the sea driven and tossed by the wind. For let not
> *that man suppose that he will receive anything from*
> *the Lord.*

God is telling us here that a doubter is someone who wavers between faith and unbelief and therefore, is unprepared to receive the very thing he seeks. Whatever God has promised the believer in His Word can only be received by faith. Doubt is a disease that eats away your faith like a cancer. Doubt is the devil's handmaid who he sends to seduce your faith and rob you of God's blessing. Faith is from God; doubt is from Satan.

How Can We Overcome the Temptation to Doubt?

Accept Christ's Atonement as Sufficient for All Your Sins

Is doubt a sin? It is one of the greatest! God's Word declares: *"But without faith it is impossible to please Him" (Heb. 11:6)*. Again, *"for whatever is not of faith is sin" (Rom. 14:23)*. Did Jesus die for all our sins? Then He also died for our doubts, because God's Word plainly states that doubt is a sin and displeases God. *"Cast you're burdens on the Lord and He will surly remove them." (I Peter 5:7)*.

When You Ask For a Promise of God Always Ask in Faith and Expect an Answer

Too often prayer goes unanswered because Christians do not really take God's integrity seriously enough to expect an answer each time they pray. They hope that occasionally their "turn" will come up and God will give them what they ask. But God is interested in answering all prayers and fulfilling His promises to us---that is why He made them. The **only requirement** is, however, that we must ask in faith, without doubting.

> *"Therefore, I say to you, whatever things you ask when you pray believe that you receive them, and you will have them." (Mk. 11:24).*

> *"If you have faith and do not doubt…whatever you ask in prayer believing, you shall receive." (Matt. 21: 21-22).*

Always Stop Doubt at the Door of the Mind When it seeks to Gain Entrance

This is where defeat always begins---*in the mind!* Satan suggests such doubts to your mind as to whether or not God is willing to answer a particular prayer request, or whether you are worthy, or have asked properly. He will tell you your problem is too difficult, or your disease too far advanced to hope for a cure. Here is where most people become defeated. They allow thoughts of doubt to enter their mind; they entertain the doubt; they examine its merits; or they try and reason with the problem instead of resting on God's promise.

We are not to ever entertain doubt about what we have prayed for. Satan will bring thoughts of doubt, but we are able to rebuke them and speak forth God's Word. We can learn to stop doubt at the door and never entertain it again. You can overcome all doubt and transform your entire Christian life. You alone hold the key to victory. Simply refuse to accept doubtful thoughts when Satan suggests them. *"Resist the devil and he will flee from you."*

28

When You Are Tempted to Doubt, Praise God, Pray in the Spirit and Sing Songs of Faith and Victory Instead

This is one of the most effect weapons the believer has against the enemy. There is nothing that will banish Satan with his lies and doubts quicker than praise and song. The devil will flee if you command him, but he will also flee if you praise God! He simply refuses to stay around Christians who continually offer praises to God. *If we would praise God more, we would have to command the devil less.*

Praise covers you with a protective garment which the spirit of depression, doubt and heaviness cannot penetrate. The Spirit of joy is, and praise is, one of the benefits Christ purchased at Calvary, because the Lord declares in Isaiah 61:1-3; *"The Spirit of the Lord is upon me…to console those who mourn in Zion…the oil of joy for mourning, the garment of praise for the spirit of heaviness…"* Israel once overcame her enemies with song and praise unto the Lord without a weapon being used or without a fight. So can you. Read II Chronicles 20

Never Confess Doubt or Unbelief

Always confess what God's Word says and hold fast to it in the face of all circumstances which appear to the contrary, for you will receive what you confess. *"Death and life are in the power of the tongue"* (James 1:6-7).

Confessing doubt invites a spirit of depression and defeat. Satan attacks the mind with thoughts of doubt and unbelief seeking to destroy your peace and your joy in the Lord because he knows that *"the joy of the Lord is your strength"* (Neh. 8:10).

One of the greatest sources of weakness, failure, unanswered prayer, and defeat in your own tongue. Speaking doubt is your own admission that you are defeated and Satan is victor! Truly "death and life are in the power of the tongue." Never allow yourself to use negative or doubtful expressions of speech.

Refuse to Listen to the Doubts of Others

Listening to the doubts, disbelief, skepticism, and uncertainty of others can undermine and weaken your faith. Never discuss any problem(s) you have committed to the Lord, or any promises of God you have requested, with anyone who does not believe God absolutely answers every prayer of faith that is based upon His Word.

Discipline yourself to a Faithful Study of God's Word and Regular Prayer

The most effective remedy for doubt is a close relationship with God. Read I Peter 2:2; Jude 2:20; and James 4:7. If you never open the door to doubt than faith will take its place. The two cannot exist together---if one is present the other is absent. The choice is yours: Faith or Doubt!

CHAPTER SIX

How To Overcome Satan By Faith

The New Testament describes the Christian life as Spiritual warfare. The Apostle Paul emphasizes this fact by admonishing us in Ephesians 6:11-12: *"Put on the whole armor of God, that you may be able to stand against the wiles of the devil* (wiles meaning tricks & strategies intended to ensnare and deceive you). *For we do not wrestle against flesh and blood, but against principalities, against powers, against rulers of the darkness of this age, against spiritual hosts of wickedness in the heavenly places."*

Scripture is full of such references about spiritual conflict which is waged against us by an evil, cunning, wicked, powerful adversary, who rules over a vast, highly organized kingdom.

The bible also predicts an increase in demonic activity at the close of the present age prior to the Second Advent. The kingdom of darkness has expanded rapidly, affecting and influencing the entire world: its governments, society, the church and even the life of the believer. It is also seen in the increase of crime, lust, deceit, immorality, suicide, war, homosexuality, fear, worry, anxiety, disease, psychic disorders, demonic possession, drug addiction, alcoholism, and the increase in occultism, and false religions.

Because the forces against the believer and the Church are spiritual, they can only be overcome by spiritual armor and spiritual weapons. The importance of faith, together with the baptism in the Holy Spirit and the manifestation of the gifts of the Spirit cannot be overemphasized.

Without faith and the empowering of the Holy Spirit the Church is practically helpless and defenseless. The mere carnal weapons of medical science, theological education, psychiatry, psychology, religion and social institutions are not sufficient nor are they largely effective. Why? Because; *"For though we walk in the flesh, we do not war according to the flesh: because the weapons of our warfare are not carnal, but mighty for pulling down strongholds"* (2 Cor. 10:3-4). (Strongholds are deceptions of the mind). Additional supporting scriptures would be Zech. 4:6 and I Peter 5:8-9.

Personal resistance to Satan's oppression, temptation, affliction, and all his work, whether he assaults your mind or body, your family or church, is a *spiritual warfare of faith.* Satan can be overcome and defeated by the use of spiritual weapons and armor made available to the believer who is to use them in faith. How is this to be accomplished? When the enemy attacks, take the offensive against him by faith in the following ways.

1. **State Your Authority Over Satan By Faith**

   As a Christian you have this authority by virtue of your relationship with Jesus Christ. In 2 Corinthians 5:14 we are told we have *"died with Christ."* In Ephesians 2:5 it says *"we are made alive with Christ;"* and in Ephesians 2:6 it says we have been *"raised up together, made to sit in heavenly places in Christ Jesus."*

Where is Jesus? This is a significant question, because wherever He is we are with Him with respect to our position of authority. So where is He? He not only lives in you but He is enthroned at the right hand of God "Far above all principality and power and might and domain" (Eph. 2:21).

Paul's prayer is that we would recognize this fact and use this great power and authority to exalt Christ and defeat Satan. Christ not only gained victory over Satan and his kingdom at Calvary but He continually rules over him, and Satan has no power over Him whatsoever. Therefore, since as believer's we are positioned with Christ, then we to have gained the same victory and power over Satan. But the first thing we must do is to *speak* it by faith and command him (the devil) to obey us.

Don't fight Satan on his terms or with carnal weapons. Began your warfare from a position of victory. Tell him you know you have authority over him and he must obey.

2. Confess Your Victory Through the Blood of Jesus

Boldly confess (speak aloud) the effectual power of Jesus' blood because the strength of our authority comes solely from His blood alone. Our word and our testimony are effective only to the extent that we know and confess this. Scripture says; *"and they shall overcome him (Satan) by the blood of the Lamb, and by the word of their testimony"* (Rev. 12:11).

Boldly confess the power of Jesus over yourself or others no matter what Satan's attack consists of. Satan will always give way when a believer pleads the power of Jesus' blood in faith. This is true if the attack is personal, against your home, against your family, against your church, against whatever and whoever. This can be accomplished by word, by song, by praise, by testimony confession, or by the exorcism of demons. We have literally heard demon spirits say they hate it when someone speaks in tongues, or confesses the blood of Christ over them in faith. This is because they know that person has power over them.

3. Command Satan to Depart in Jesus Name

Satan will not depart, nor desist his destructive work by a polite request for him to go. The Scriptures teach us that demons are to be **cast out**, not requested to leave.

Mark 16:17 says; *"And these signs will follow those who believe. In My name they will cast out demons…"* Jesus and the Apostles rebuked evil spirits and commanded them to leave regardless of the nature of their oppression, whether a spirit of *infirmity* (Lk. 4:38-39; Mk. 9:25); *an unclean spirit* (Mk. 1:23-27); *temptation* (Mk. 10:4a); *hindrance* (Mt. 16:21; 23); or *interference* (Acts 16:16-18).

Too many Christians ignore their authority over the enemy. I have heard believers say; "I would be afraid to say anything to Satan. I would rather ignore him"! This, of course, gives Satan complete liberty to work unmolested in that person's life. **You, as a believer, have the authority to set yourself and others free from Satan's bondage, but he will only leave with a direct command of faith in Jesus' name.**

Christians must understand that Satan and his demonic forces know they have been defeated by Christ and His followers have authority over them. But our victory is not automatic…it only comes when we come to know and believe we have this authority to the extent we act on it (Jam. 2:19; Lk. 10:17; Mk. 16:17).

4. Use the Shield of Faith and the Sword of the Spirit

Jesus overcame Satan's temptation with Scripture saying, "it is written." Then the apostle Paul admonishes us in Ephesians 6:16 by saying; *"Above all, take up the shield of faith with which you are able to quench the fiery darts of the wicked one."*

Notice that one weapon is a defensive weapon (shield of faith), and the other is an offensive weapon (the sword of the Spirit). These two weapons together can overcome any assault of Satan. We simply have to maintain our faith by speaking what God's Word promises and Satan will be compelled to remove his work of oppression.

5. Resist Satan in Faith

There are numerous scriptures that tell us not to give place to the devil, resist the devil and he will flee, stand against the wiles of the devil, put on the full armor of God and wrestle against the enemy, and overcome him by the word of your testimony.

Satan's temptations and work are not to go unchallenged and unopposed. We are commanded to resist him, to stand against him, to give him no place, and to wrestle with him in prayer and faith. The devil was defeated at Calvary and has no right to whatsoever in your life, your home, or your church to oppress, hinder or defeat. Tell him he is trespassing on God's property, resist him, and demand that he depart.

6. Keep a Close Watch on Your Heart and Mind

As a believer you must refuse the entrance into your heart and mind of anything that is negative, resentful, or depressive; this is where the enemy usually strikes.

Failure to guard against Satan's depressive, carnal, sinful and negative thoughts is one major cause for oppression, sickness, disease, fear, strife, dissention, depression, despair and frustration. Why is this? Because *"...the carnal mind is enmity against God"* (Rom. 8:7). (Enmity means hatred or ill will).

If Christians would center their attention on Christ and seek to have His mind created in them, a large percentage of their current difficulties and problems just might dissolve.

7. One Last Thought

Never confess Satan's power. Only confess your power and authority in the name of Jesus based upon your position with Him.

CHAPTER SEVEN

How To Pray The Prayer Of Faith

One of the conditions set forth in Chapter Two for receiving the promises of God was that we must *ask*. We receive only what we appropriate by faith in prayer. Faith is the envelop in which every request to God must be placed. Often you will hear Christians say, "I have asked and asked but I still have not received." Why is this? One reason is that many do not know how to pray the prayer of faith. Jesus' own disciples confessed they needed to be taught how to pray, when they asked, "Lord, teach us to pray" (Lk. 11:1).

There is always a correct way to accomplish anything we undertake in order to receive the desired result. This is also true of prayer. Failure to realize this could be why many prayers are ineffective and remain unanswered. The scriptures teach us that there are certain essential principles of prayer which we must observe if our prayers are to be effective.

Prayer Must Start with Honoring God

When the disciples asked the Lord to teach them to pray (Lk. 11:1) the very first thing He mentions in verse 2 was how to begin in prayer. It was to honor our heavenly Father. Jesus said to them; *"When you pray, say: Our Father in heaven, Hallowed be Your name"*. Therefore, when we pray we should first honor our heavenly Father.

Pray with a Repentant Heart

Confession is the second requirement for effective prayer. You need to remove, by confession, any obstacles of sin or unfaithfulness which may constitute a barrier between you and the Lord. David said *"If I regard iniquity in my heart, the Lord will not hear me" (Psalm 66:18)*. James speaks of the necessity of confession in connection with prayer for healing the sick *(Jam. 5:14-16)*. See also I John 1:8-10; 3:20-22. Unconfessed sin, whether of the spirit, such as pride, selfishness, doubt, hate, etc., or sins of the flesh can cause a hindrance to your prayers.

Pray with a Forgiving Spirit

Effective prayer comes from a right relationship between you and your brother as well as between you and God. Jesus, after explaining the principles of the prayer of faith in Mark 11:22-24, then continues teaching in verses 25-26 saying, *"and whenever you stand praying, if you have anything against anyone, forgive him that your Father in heaven may also forgive you your trespasses."*

Often time's prayers are not answered because of the failure to observe this condition set forth by Jesus. Anger, enmity, hate, resentment and an unforgiving spirit toward another will imprison your prayers with walls too high for your petitions to rise above.

Pray in the Name of Jesus

It is only through Christ that we have access to the Father, *"for through Him we...have access by one Spirit unto the Father"(Eph. 2:18)*. We are also told in scripture: *"whatever you do in word or deed, do all in the name of the Lord Jesus, giving thanks to the Father through Him (Col 3:17)*. And Jesus said *"...whatever you ask the Father in My name He will give you..."(Jn. 16:23-24)*.

Pray According to the Will of God

Obviously God cannot answer a prayer contrary to His will. John says, *"And this is the confidence that we have in Him, that, if we ask anything according to His will, He hears us. And if we know that He hears us, whatever we ask, we know that we have the petitions that we have asked Him" (1 Jn. 5:14-15)*. This indicates the importance of the first condition for receiving by faith that we discussed in Chapter Two. That is, we must base our faith on what God has promised in His Word.

Pray with Expectation

It should be evident that if we are to pray the prayer of faith we _must pray expecting an answer,_ yet there are many who fail at this point. <u>Praying in faith is simply believing that</u> <u>God will do what He promises in His Word</u>. You can pray with only as much faith as you have in Christ Himself and are willing to trust Him. To the extent you believe in Him---this is the extent of your faith.

God will do what He promises He will do. Prayer only knocks on the door; faith is the key that unlocks it!

Faith is........

Faith is believing God will do what He promises He will do in scripture.

Faith is trusting God and confessing His Word rather than your circumstances.

Faith is asking God and not doubting.

Faith is resisting the negative thoughts of Satan and speaking the promises of God.

Faith is expecting an answer when you pray, knowing that God has already said yes.